ALEX ALLAN

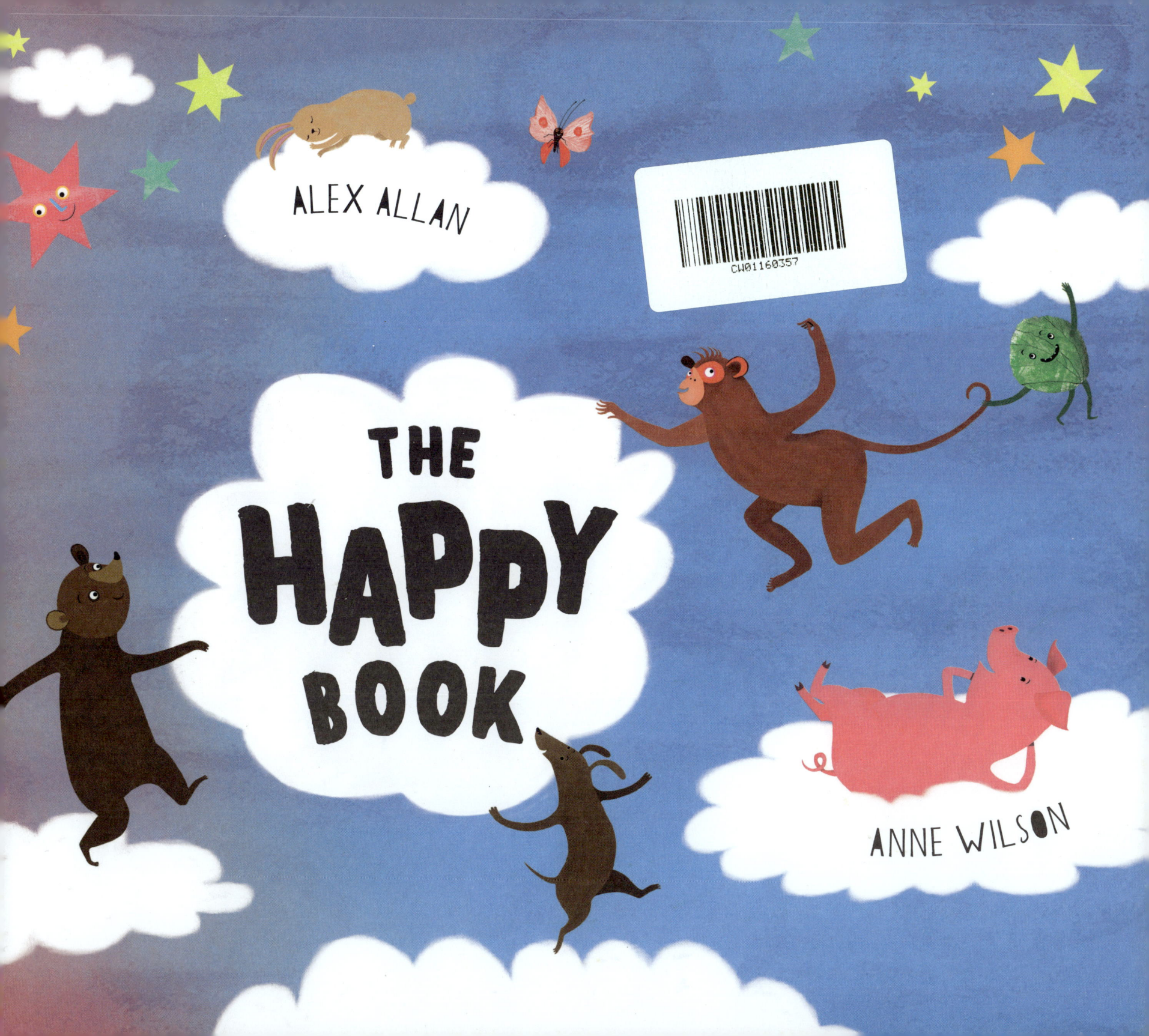

THE HAPPY BOOK

ANNE WILSON

Published in 2020 by Welbeck Children's Books
An imprint of Welbeck Children's Limited,
part of Welbeck Publishing Group
20 Mortimer Street, London W1T 3JW

Text, design and illustration © Welbeck Children's Limited, part of Welbeck Publishing Group 2020

All rights reserved. No part of this publication may be reproduced, stored in a retrieval system, or transmitted in any form or by any means, electronically, mechanical, photocopying, recording or otherwise, without the prior permission of the copyright owners and the publishers.

Designer: Claire Clewley
Design Manager: Emily Clarke
Editor: Jenni Lazell
Consultant: Sarah Davis
Production: Nicola Davey

A CIP catalogue record for this book is available from the British Library.

ISBN: 978-1-78312-546-3

Printed in China
9 8 7 6 5 4 3 2 1

Consultant Sarah Davis is a child psychotherapist, with an MA in Integrative Child and Adolescent Psychotherapy and Counselling.

Sarah has been the Young Person's Mental Health Lead for a charity in Hackney and has worked as a children's editor and consultant.

How do you feel today?

HAPPY — PAGES 4–11

SAD — PAGES 12–17

ANGRY — PAGES 18–21

SCARED — PAGES 22–25

WORRIED — PAGES 26–29

Ways to Feel Happy — PAGES 30–31

Resources for Parents and Carers — PAGE 32

HAPPY

is an emotion that looks like

this...

...and feels like SUNSHINE

...and DAISIES

...and GIGANTIC ice cream sundaes.

Things that might make you happy include:

Scoring a goal

Winning a prize

A cute puppy or kitten or rabbit

Going to a fun fair

Playing with friends

Can you think of any others?

The Science bit

When you are happy, your brain releases a chemical called dopamine

"doh-pah-meen"

that helps you to learn, remember and helps you s l e e p well.

So being **HAPPY** is good for you, right?

Sometimes when you're **happy** things are so funny you just have to **laugh** and

laugh

HA HA HA

Hee Hee Hee

Things that might make you laugh include:

A funny book or movie

Grown-ups dancing

Jokes jokes jokes (do you know any?)

Making funny faces

A pig wearing rollerskates

Being tickled (if you're ticklish!)

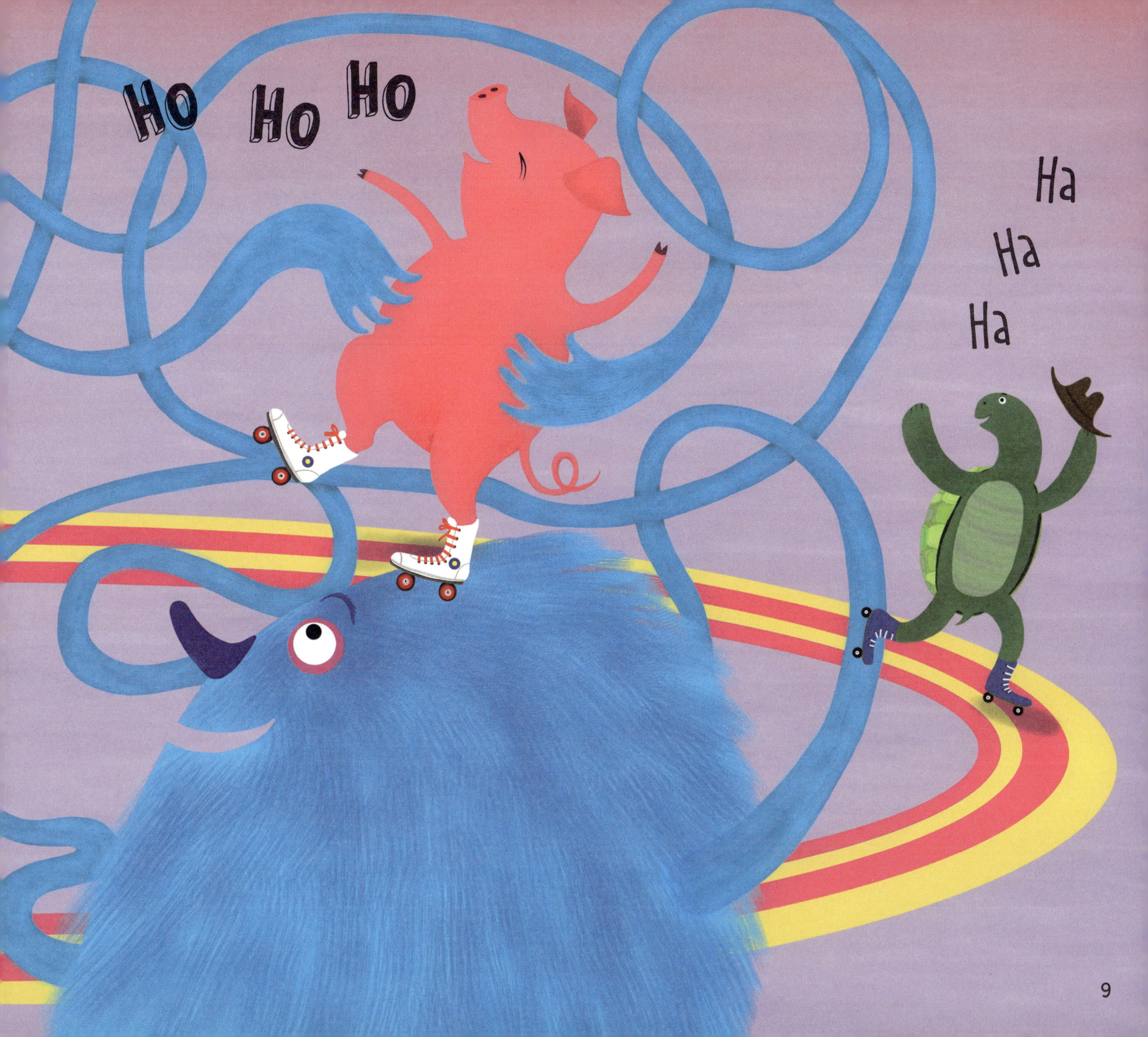
HO HO HO
Ha
Ha
Ha

What's the **funniest** thing you've ever seen?

The Science bit

When you laugh your brain releases chemicals called endorphins "en-dor-fins", which are the body's natural feel-good medicine, so laughing actually makes you feel better.

Top Tip

Have a laughing contest with a friend! Take turns to try to make each other laugh – the one who can hold off laughing for the longest wins!

We don't always feel happy and sometimes it's okay to be

SAD

Sad feels empty and

LONELY

like a wet day with no one to play

SADNESS can feel HEAVY like a stone.

Being around chopped onions can also make you cry!

Nobody knows exactly why we cry but some scientists think it's so other people know we're SAD.

But tears aren't all about feeling bad – your body makes tears all the time to stop your eyes drying out and to wash away dirt or grit.

The Science bit

When you're sad, your brain releases a chemical called acetylcholine "ay-set-ah-co-lin" which causes tears to form. Crying makes your brain release the feel-good endorphins that will help you start to feel better...

...so CRYING is also a SUPERPOWER!

What's the Matter?

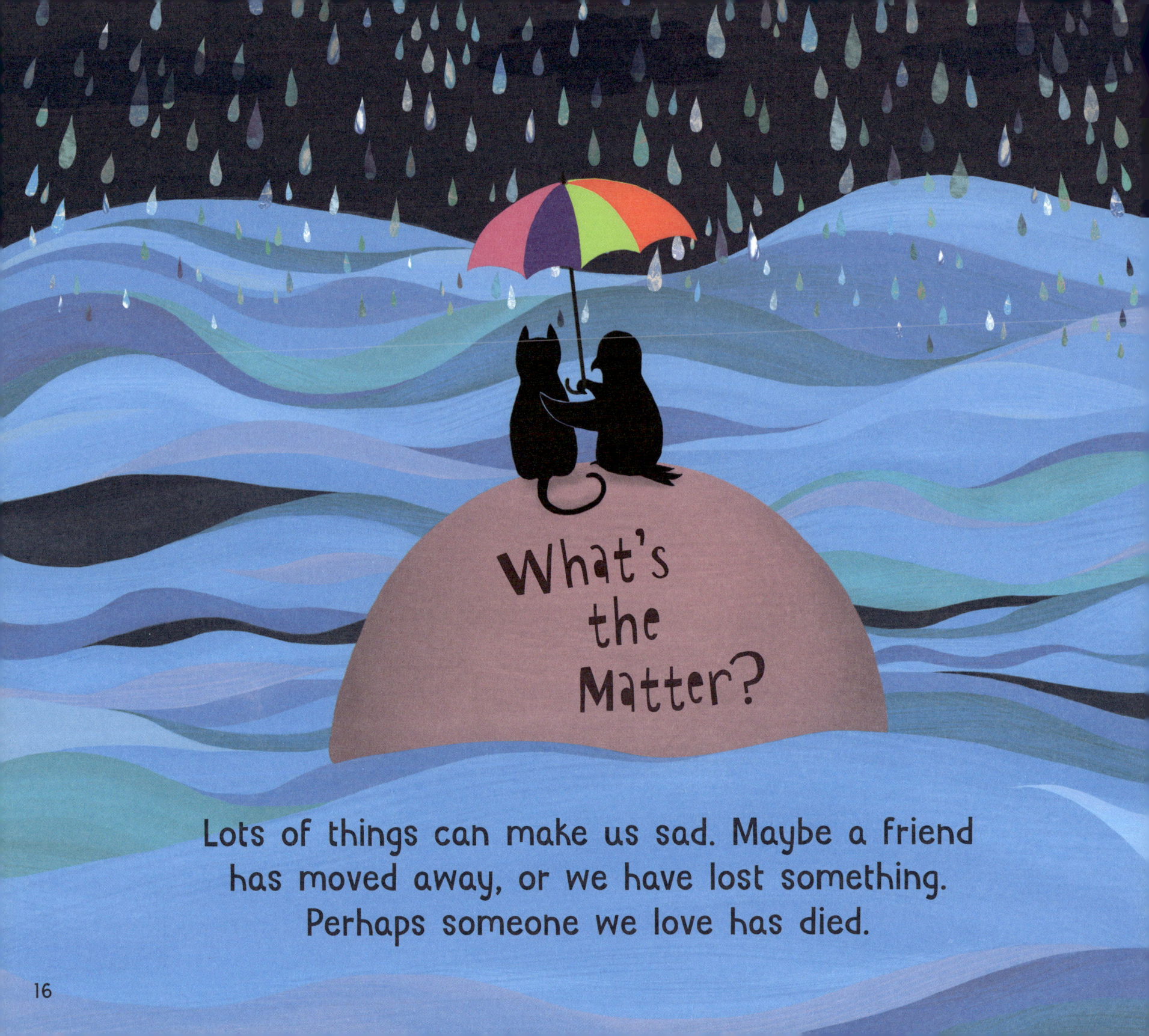

Lots of things can make us sad. Maybe a friend has moved away, or we have lost something. Perhaps someone we love has died.

Talking about and remembering the good times with family and friends can help you get through the sad times.

Things you can do if you see someone is sad:
- Try to cheer them up
- Ask them what's wrong
- Be patient and listen
- Offer to help

What makes you feel better when you are crying?

Have you ever felt like you are going to **BUBBLE** and **BUBBLE** and **BOIL** over like a kettle with steam coming out of your ears?

ANGRY feels RED HOT and SPIKY

When you're angry, you might say: It's not fair! It's not my fault! I HATE you!

The Science bit

When you get angry, your brain sends a chemical called adrenaline

"ah-dren-ah-lin"

through your body, and this causes your heart to race and your breathing to get faster. Some people go red in the face and they clench their fists!

Think of your angry brain like a dog barking and snapping, and try to soothe it with gentle words and slow breathing.

"Down boy"

Once you're calmer it's easier to talk about what is making you angry.

What can you do if you start to feel angry?

1... Take deep breaths and relax your muscles

2... Get some fresh air

3...

4... Pause and count to 10

5...

Sometimes it's hard to feel happy because something is making you

SCARED

Scary Stuff:

The dark

Thunder and lightning

Putting up your hand in school

Feeling lonely or left out

Monsters under the bed

Trying something new

FEAR can feel a bit like anger. You might feel your heart beating faster, your breath getting shorter and you might start to

shake
and
tremble.

The Science bit

When you're scared you might want to scream and shout, or you might just want to run away! Don't worry, it's normal to feel this way. It is called your

FIGHT or FLIGHT

response and it's your body's way of protecting you from danger.

WHAT CAN YOU DO IF YOU'RE FEELING SCARED?

Like most things, it helps to talk about it. Once you know what your fear is, you can work out what to do about it. Sometimes it's good to face your fears head on

but sometimes it's okay to run away too, and let an adult tackle the problem.

Was it something I said?

Top Tip

Facing a fear might seem terrifying, but it can be really helpful too. Try tackling one of your fears! Once you've done it you'll feel more confident next time. (TAKE THAT, YOU MEAN BEANS!)

When you ignore your fears they can pile up and get BIGGER and BIGGER. Before you know it you can be worrying about them ALL THE TIME and this can make you feel bad.

WORRIES

Signs that you are worried might include:

Finding it hard to speak

Biting your fingernails

Butterflies in your tummy

Chewing your sleeve (yuck!)

Tightness in your throat

Worries usually start out small so it's best to deal with them before they get any BIGGER.

You could write your worries down...

It can help to talk about your worries — a problem shared is a problem halved.

...or imagine them as leaves being tossed into a river and

floating away...

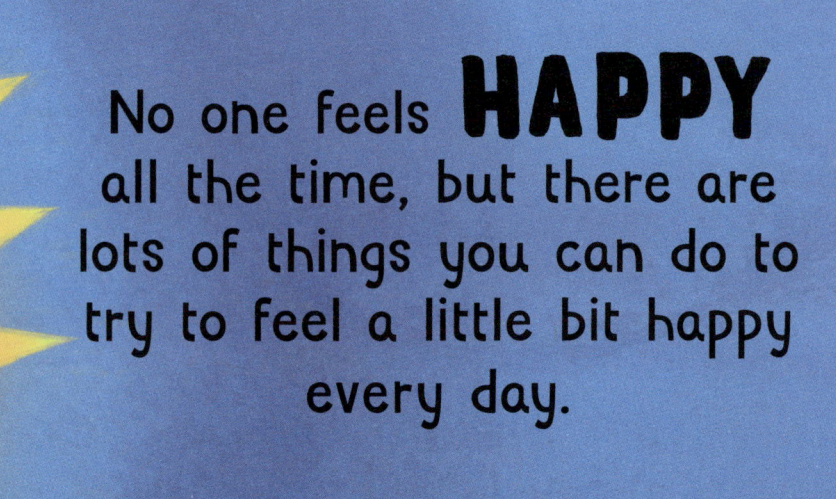

No one feels **HAPPY** all the time, but there are lots of things you can do to try to feel a little bit happy every day.

TALK about what's making you feel bad

stay **ALTIVE** to release endorphins

Showing kindness and helping others can feel just as good as when something nice is done for you. You could start by helping someone at school or helping with chores at home.

BE KIND

REACH OUT

get enough SLEEP so you have more energy

RESOURCES FOR PARENTS AND CARERS

For help and advice about staying happy and healthy, please see the following resources:

www.place2be.org.uk
www.actionforhappiness.org
www.zerotothree.org
www.youngminds.org.uk